HER STORY...

Created for a Time Like This

Hazel Ford

ISBN 978-1-64569-799-2 (paperback)
ISBN 978-1-64569-800-5 (digital)

Christian Faith Publishing, Inc.
832 Park Avenue
Meadville, PA 16335
www.christianfaithpublishing.com

Printed in the United States of America

To the real loves of my life, my dear children who have seen me go through so many hard times and struggles. They were witnesses to the ups and downs, and I'm sure they went through these struggles along with me.

I had so many issues being a single parent, sometimes not knowing which way to go or sometimes not knowing what to do. There were many times I would lay on my bed and cry, trying to be so very careful not to let them hear me; I had to try to remain strong in front of them as to not let them worry. I was not a perfect mother, but I knew that it was my duty to raise them. I look at them now, and I can say that I am so proud of the way that they grew and became the adults they are today. There is not a day that I don't pray for them. I want them to know that I love them with all my heart. I will forever ask that they will forgive me. I'm so grateful that they blessed me with eleven (great) grandkids who are number one in my life. Each and every time I see them, it's like getting a surprise.

My children are my heroes. They have taught me so many things about how to be a great parent and how to be more patient. They also showed me about life after the struggle they've endured along with me. I can boldly say, "Look at my children now. I'm so proud, so very proud of you."

From Mom
From Grandma with love
To God be the glory

Hello, my heavenly Father who art in heaven, it is you that is holy and righteous. There is none like you. I'm so glad that you know me. You are God who forgives, but you won't forgive me unless I forgive others. I have a few issues, but you already know that. Father, I ask you to forgive me. Work on me as only you can. There is none who can work on me, heal me, deliver me, take control over my life but you. Help me to forgive as you so willingly forgive me. I've held on to so much for so long it's time to let it all go.

Thank you,
Your child

Acknowledgments

To my best friend, Ms. Tina Watson:

Y ou have been on my side for the longest time. Her words of encouragement mean so much to me. She has been my biggest cheerleader since I started writing my story. I thank God for putting her in my life. I found out that I could speak openly to her about anything. I am thankful that Tina has been my biggest fan. I want to say thank you for being my friend, my prayer partner, and my shoulder to cry on. You have done so much for me. I am grateful for every favor that you have done out of heart felt love for me.

To Porta Sturdivant (my niece):

To my very own niece, Portia, who, out of her busy schedule took time out of her day for me. All the time that she put in to type my story is priceless. I will forever be grateful. Knowing that she didn't have to do it, but she did, means so very much to me.

Thank you for taking time to correct my errors. I will never forget how you came home from work and still made time for me. Thank you for being patient with me and making the changes that were needed. You even had the foresight to further understand the points I was trying to make. I could even call you my partner in the story. I will always remember what you did for me.

I thank my God for you being in place when I called on you. You were like my own personal summons (LOL). I can most certainly say that it must have been a part of the plan that God had in mind. Thank you for your perfect labor of love. Thank you in the name of the Father, the Son, and the Holy Spirit.

With lots of love,
Your Aunt Hazel

Introduction

Where did all of this come from? How did all of this come about? I didn't know what you were doing. I was a little girl! What are you doing? Why am I being covered up? Why couldn't anyone see me to stop it? Did you know what that was? I was a little girl!

I heard you say, "Get out of my way," but what did I do? You pushed me aside when you were done, but what did that mean? You pushed me out of your way. I felt broken, but what is *broken*? What does that mean?

"I'll just run away and leave you on the floor." Where did you go? What does that mean?

Alone. Pushed to the side. "Get out of my way!" But I was just a little girl! What does that mean? I didn't know if I was loved or not. I didn't understand love. How can you be loved if no one can see you? I was always hidden. I felt ashamed, but how did I know what that meant? I was a little girl! I thought that I had no one. I was gone. I was not there. I was not here. Can you see me? I was gone.

You see, this is the mind of a little girl who was raped. But not by someone she doesn't know, but her brother.

I don't know where any of this will go, but someone needs to know. Maybe your little girl or boy. I ask this question, "Have you asked them?" No one knew to ask me when I was just a little girl. But you know. I found out that there is no weapon that is formed against me that shall prosper according to God's word. You see, I didn't know this. I didn't know that God was with me, but He was. This weapon was meant to shut me down, tear me apart. It was supposed to rape and destroy my vision my hope, my love. The enemy was trying to come against me with everything in him, but I can truly say, "But God." I didn't know that there was a turnaround place for me. You see, I was just a little girl. There was a time I used to think that I couldn't be seen, and I used to wonder why. I used to act out so that I could be seen. I was mean, I was hateful, I was so ashamed, not even understanding shame. I didn't even know why. I didn't know what was going on, and I repeat, I was just a little girl.

You mainly wouldn't think of molestation as a weapon. You see, when most people think of weapons, we usually think of knives or a gun. Anything that can cause us to be broken, torn apart, hurt, or anything to cause you to want to hurt yourself or other people can be used as a weapon. Anything that will cause you to lose who you are. Anything that will try to cause you to lose who you are or even try to take your future. Anything that can make you forget who you are or even cause you to feel so shy until it stops your growth is a weapon.

There are so many boys and girls who go through this sort of thing every day and still not understand. They have been groomed to this and think that it is somehow normal, but it's not, and it's not okay at all.

If I could, I would ask, "How did you become what you were?" What would be your story?

It makes me wonder where did it come from. If I could ask you, I can almost hear you telling the same story. You were not even a grown man, you were still a very young teenager. In my mind, I can hear you say, "I want to be satisfied, but when I'm done, get out of my way." You feel something you're not supposed to feel. I push you away. "Stop that, little girl, what are you doing? Stay here in the dark. You are a bad little girl." Pushed aside, all broken and confused. What does that mean? Just left under the covers, in the dark. The weapon was the darkness.

I really hope that what has been said will open someone's eyes and be a help to them. The story doesn't stop here. It's time to tell your own story. Together we can tell the little girls and boys that it's okay for them to come out of their dark place.

Where Do I Belong?

I will be glad when I find my way out. I found out that my healing is in my forgiving. That's the key, so glad that I found that out. The little girl is waiting to be healed. But what after my healing? Will she be the same? First little girl is healed. You thought they were the same, but they weren't. Now go and get her, tell her it's okay for her to grow up and be alright.

Didn't you see me? I didn't see you coming. You were just there. You said, "Let's go play." I never saw you coming. Why could you not see me? What was that you showed me? How is it I never saw you coming? Why did you always cover me up and said that this is play? Little girl, small little girl waiting to grow. It's time for you to come and get me. The other little girl is healed. Now it's my turn. You forgot about me.

First little girl was healed and set free. She had a loud cry. She cried so loudly until she got your attention. With that being said, her mother and her were set free. You see little girl, your mother couldn't see you because she couldn't see herself. She was beaten, battered, and broken. She couldn't see the light; her hope was gone. Where there is no light and only darkness, you can't see anything. She wasn't trying to hurt me, but she couldn't see me. You can't see if you are blind. The enemy, my father, stripped her of all hope. So she killed herself by her own hands, by my father's hands.

You were so glad to be free. You forgot about me. Young sick boy, not even knowing how sick you were. But how could you? Damaged kids, mother, and father. Makes me wonder what was going on. Had to be the work of the weapon. Now I can say, if it had not been for the Lord who was on my side, where would I be? God knows every heart. Even the heart of yours, little girl. Precious little girl, I wasn't big enough to help you or myself. But I am now. You see, the enemy didn't have the power to keep me small. He didn't have the power to keep me hidden under the covers. He didn't count on me finding my way out of the dark place I was in. But God! Had it not been for the Lord, who was on my side, He showed me His love and mercy. He kept me through all of my hurts. Even the things that I thought was normal. Whenever a little already hurt, a child is told that this is play, and the child believes that. They have been trained to believe the devil's lies. He took the word *play* and turned it into his weapon. He must've forgotten that no weapon formed against me shall prosper.

Getting in Position
(Jeremiah 18:2)

etting in position to stand-up position to walk position to pull-back-the-covers position to open-the-door position to come-out position to open her mouth and speak, and let the darkness know your time is up! You dead thing, you lose. I'm the winner. I'm the child of the Most High God. I'm in position to tell your story, little girl. So that some other little girl, boy, woman, or man will know that there is a way out. It's your turn.

I can pray for you—and I do pray for you—but I can't save you. I love you, but I can't save you. I can encourage you, but I can't save you. I can stand by you, but I can't stand for you. You see, I was there too. So many hurts, but I was there too. This is where I say, "Let God be God, you just pray." Taking the covers off and bits and pieces. I want to see your face. I never saw you, but I have seen enough to tell my story. I was always hidden away from everyone. But I know someone else has this story, and we can agree.

I see you now, I see you, little girl. You can come out. Do you remember the day you stood up and said, "Stop!" when it became clear to me what was being done? You got big enough and used your voice. You took back from the abuser yourself, but the little girl didn't—not yet.

You see, hurting people sometimes want to hurt back. Little boy, little hurt and sad child, you hurting me didn't stop your hurt. I have been relieved of everything that has to do with bondage. No longer bound, not chained. You tried to destroy a little girl, but I came to uncover her so that she can see her way. You see, I got big enough. Your reign is over, devil, and she wins. She now knows who God is, and "devil," you lost. My duty is to pray and let God be God.

There is someone who's waiting for your help, little girl. You are big enough now. She is waiting on you. The hurts and tragedies were meant to destroy the family as a whole. The young boy rapist and the father rapist were all a big lie to say that God is not God. You tried to leave me in this great big world to say that I have no hope, and that's a lie also. I'm out of my sick bed now. It's time for me to wake up some more sick people.

Come on, little girl, let's walk on Satan's head with the word of God. Because God is God, now let's shout about it. Your reign is over. Satan, you are the one who robs, steals, and destroy. Third chapter of Ecclesiastes says to everything there is a season, a time for every purpose under heaven and a purpose for everything under heaven. And I say it in my own words, "My time to be freed up from my past." My time to be healed. My time to rejoice. My time to go and get my little girl. My time to praise the Lord. My time to forgive. Not that it makes it alright, but forgiveness is for your own peace. This time is your time. This freedom is meant for you. This is your time to move on. My time to just be glad and it's about that time. My time to even forgive me. Your time is up, Satan. Your reign has come to an end. Your power has ended. I don't have the spirit of fear because that's not what God has given me. He gave me the spirit of power, the spirit of love, and the spirit of a sound mind.

I'm Mad at You

I want you to know that I am angry with you. You were mean. You were not kind. You did not care. Did you not know that I was there? Could you not see me? I think you loved us because I heard you say it from time to time, but what did that mean? Being raised up in a house such as this, you took away my mother by her own hands. When you looked at her, what did you see? You couldn't see a wife? You couldn't see a mother? You couldn't see me at all? I needed a mother to show me the way, but what did you see? Why were you so angry?

I can see clearly now why she did what she did. It seems to me she saw death as a way out. No wonder she killed herself. That's because death was better than what you were putting her through. I went through so much at that time. I saw and did not understand. How could anyone do such a thing to a child? What were you thinking? I carried this pain in my heart for so many years. I thought I would never get past it. How could you ever allow me to experience such a thing? You didn't even care that I saw you. You never confessed or said you were sorry about anything. But the curse is broken now. And I take my power back from you. No more control from the grave. You no longer have control over me. Because you were hurting also, let me say, "I forgive you." So maybe you can rest now, hurt little boy who grew into a hurting man.

Oh, Who Do You Love? Not Me

Self-hatred.

You know for a long time I hated myself? I didn't like me. I hated my name. I hated my life, and I wanted something to change. I thought if I got married, that would somehow change me. Because your name connected me to you. But thanks be to God, He put an end to all of that.

New?

Different name, same person.

New name but still empty. New name, same heart. New name, same hurt. New name, same issues. The new name was supposed to hide me, but it couldn't because it did not know what direction I was supposed to go in. New name, still broken. I didn't like her, she was too broken. Why was she so broken? The enemy wanted to break and defeat me to hide what God has put in me.

As I look back after so many years, I can see the great things that God has put in me. One of them is music, and poetry is another, just to name a few. This is not including the gifts of my children and grandchildren. I could have gone so far, but it's still not too late. At times, I paddled. Sometimes I dragged myself along. I even had to hold on to broken pieces to stay afloat. But somehow, I made it. Still there are scares, but Satan, you failed. You see, I still made it because there is a balm in Gilead. His name is Jesus. Satan, you no longer have a dwelling place. The little girl knows she is okay. She is no longer covered up.

Stand up, little girl. So much I couldn't see. I didn't know where I was. I got lost. But I had to go back to get me. Hey, I found you, little girl. Give me your hand, little girl, you are not alone anymore. I was always there, but I couldn't see me. So I'm glad that you came back. Stand up, little girl. You can walk, so walk in the power of God. You were shaken but not destroyed.

Stuck in One Spot

She got stuck in one place, but where was that place? It was always dark. How did I get there? How did I get out? I don't even remember standing up. I don't remember seeing a door. But you know, I don't want to remember anything else. I'm just glad that you came back to get me. You kept me on your mind as if you were watching over me. I'm glad you came to get me.

Sick Little Girl

I'm so glad that God was on my side because where would I be had it not been for Him? So glad that you saved me. So glad that you saw me. So glad that you kept me. I didn't know it at that time. You brought me out when I was so sick and all I could do is just lay there. I tried to breath. I don't know how I even lived. Many times, I saw death coming for me and I waited. But it still couldn't reach me, but I waited. I was a little girl trying to die. But what did that mean? I didn't know what that meant. But I knew that the sickness would end. When my mother was alive, she would take me to the doctor, but you took her away. What did you see when you came over to the bed and looked at me? Could you see me? And what was in your heart? Maybe you were hurting for me. I think you felt my pain. Because you were my father, you had to be hurting too. I want to forgive you, and I do. But I never in all these years even grieved your passing. I just didn't think to grieve over you. Your passing is just what it was. I'm looking forward to saying that I love you and I forgive you.

To my brother, my sick brother...I don't wonder anymore about you, I just want to forgive you. You no longer have control because sometimes hurt people will a lot of the time want to hurt others. Even though you gave your life to God in later years as you said, I can believe that. When you got sick, I never heard your cry or complain about anything. I heard someone say that when you were ready to go, you told him, "I'm ready now." You marched into the kingdom to your rest (good job). I really didn't mourn you. I don't know if I even cried, but I know that you were saved and God called you home and it's time for me to stand up. Thy will be done, oh God.

Holding On to Dead Things

Dead things can't talk unless you give it your voice to use. Dead things can't walk unless you give it your legs. Dead things can't think unless you give it a place in your mind. Dead things can't hold on to you unless you give it your hand and also give it a reason. Dead things can't move in on you unless you give it a place to stay.

God, you gave me a message some time ago. I thought it was for someone else, but it's coming clear that it's for me as well. I'm tired of dead things. Dead thing, your time is up. Enemy your time is up. Enemy your grave is dug. It's time for you to be in the dark now. You tried to make me think that I was lost. You tried to make me think that I was nothing. You tried to shape me into something that was not real. You tried to change my whole outlook on life. (But God) I can now say, if it had not been for the Lord who was on my side, where would I be? Just like you hated me with all that was in you, God loves me more than that, you dead thang. Because Jesus loves me, I always had the power. But the power I had didn't look like power. Nobody told me that I had it. But where would this power take me? You see, I don't know where it will lead me, but I believe it will keep me standing still in God.

I had to learn to love my life, I just didn't know it. The enemy wanted to take my life, but he couldn't. By the power that was in me, my power was in God. The enemy wanted to stop my growth. (But God) He wanted to block the joy in my life. (But God) He wanted me to keep on hating myself. (But God) I wanted to die. (But God) It was impossible for me to be dead unless God said so.

There was a time when I thought I had nothing to do and nowhere to go. The sky above me was quiet. The ground under me was hard. People around me couldn't see me.

One day as we were talking, one of my friends said to me at one point in my life that she didn't know I went through anything because I didn't look like it. She never even asked what was going on or even did I need to talk. I was going through the same hurts as so many others but didn't know what to do about it. It made me think why I was even alive. (But God) How can you call on anyone for help when no one can see you? I now can say, "God, what was that all about?" You must've had a reason. What was the meaning of it all? I never found the door so that I can come out. That's why the little girl couldn't come out. But she had to come and remind me to come and get her. You left me in such a big world to make it on my own. Somehow, I made it. I want to learn how to love. I want to learn how to live. I want to learn how to trust. I want to learn how to use my voice. Someone needs what I have. They need to know how to come out. Someone else has this same story, just waiting for me to get up.

Where Were You?

Who are you? I don't know the person in the casket. Who was that? I never saw you like that. No one explained anything to me. They pushed me along so quickly, I couldn't see you. So many people. What does all of this mean? They didn't say anything. Was I the only one there? Where were all of the people? And where were you? I couldn't remember your face. I was so sad. I'm sorry I was always in your way. But where was I? Where did I go? But you know my mother, that part doesn't hurt anymore. I survived. I just had to go and get the little hurt girl, so she would be all right. I know you couldn't see me because all your vision was stripped away. You just wanted to run to safety. Not because you didn't love us, because you did. You were just so broken. Even your vision of life was shattered. I miss you. I love you. I'm glad that you are at rest. I learned so much from you. Even though I don't remember your face, I still remember you. I would follow you around all the time. I even cook like you now. I used to watch you all of the time. I don't understand how I forgot your face, but I remember you.

So Amazing

Somehow, we don't know one another, but I see that most of our stories are so much alike. Some of our stories are the same. It's time to speak out and take back our power. Now it's time for change. I am so tired of it all. Spirit of hurt, I'm tired of you. Spirit of pain, your time is up. Spirit of darkness, the covers are pulled off you. Spirit of crying, you are dried up. So *stop*! I call you what you are in the name of Jesus. Spirit of sorrow, you are no more. Spirit of confusion, *go*! The little girl, that's not who she is. I came back. I came and got her, and her light is shining again. All of the covers have been pulled back. Hey, little girl, you are free. Satan is defeated. God is living. So get up and go tell someone how you were set free. Go in the name of Jesus. Let your beauty shine. Let it shine. Open your mouth and speak. Someone needs to hear you. It's your turn now go.

I Just Want to Praise You

S o grateful that you allowed me to praise you. Thank you for giving me back my joy. I'm even glad for the rain today. I'm glad for the cold. Just glad to be here. Thank you, Lord, for my peace. So blessed, so very blessed. I'm waiting for something new to happen in my life. Don't know what that is, but I'm still waiting. Wonder what that would be like?

Ruined and Broken Spirits

Ruined—total destruction, broken in pieces, out of order, imperfect, ill, dispirited, to be turned around with blinders on, not knowing which to go, in a state of confusion, crippled without any help, dazed state, can't see, can't go forward, can't see how to get up, punished without cause, empty.

Now where do I go from here? I have no more time for this. Too much time has been wasted. I had to be reminded that it was time to get up. Enemy, you were just for a little while, but my God is forever. Your spirit has been broken. You can no longer arise in me. It's *over*! You shadow of what was is no more. Time for you to go. Move out! I take back my power. Satan, you lost. The little girl is on her way out. You tried to hide my help from me. But my help sits high and looks low. When I thought I couldn't be seen, He saw me all the time. I'm moving away from what was familiar to me because God came and got me. You wanted me to think that if I kept it hidden, then no one would know but you and me. You forgot we aren't friends. You are my enemy. You tried a little girl and even me when I was young but look at God and what he can do. I have no more reason to cry. Just like God came and got me when it was time, He will do the same for others who have been hurt. So I say, let God be God. You just pray, little girl.

I Thought I Was Broken

Broken—taken apart, disassembled, some here, some there, some lost behind something, some hidden, fallen apart but still here.

I have eyes that I might see you better, and I do. I have my legs that I might be able to walk, and I can. I still have my arms and I can hug and be hugged. I have a mouth, and I learned how to speak God's word. I was shaken, but I didn't break. Little girl, you are not broken. You have a story to tell. There are so many little girls like you, and they need to hear your voice. You have something to say. Abuse wanted to stop you. Hurting was trying to hold you back. Sadness wanted to keep you crying. Darkness wanted to keep you hid. Anger wanted to keep you fighting. I was lonely and that caused me not to trust. You say talk, but talk to who? Anybody. Everybody—the young, the old, men, women, boys and girls. Tell it all, they need to be made free.

Not a Place of Comfort

My father, you were not a place of comfort because you didn't know comfort. You were not a place of peace because you didn't know peace. How you must have been hurt to make you choose to hurt. Why were you so angry at her all of the time? Why was my brother so mixed up? Why did you become the enemy to the family? The Bible says to train up a child in the way that he should go and when he is old, he would not depart from it. Is that what you thought it meant? You were way off. You can't blame drinking on that. You know the child that is yours even when drunk. But you are gone now. I always wanted to say all of this and more to you. But as I grew, I kind of lost track of life trying to live but just getting by.

Today is the day that I get around to telling you I don't like you. But I bet you don't like you either. But I must forgive you, and I do because you can no longer be a part of me.

With love, the little girl and me.

I can't keep looking back at you and looking forward at the same time. That's it!

Locked In

You tried to turn me into someone that was not me. That was not my role in life. Is that who you saw when you looked at that picture? I could only be me. You tried to hide me behind someone else's life that did not belong to me. I was just a little girl. The enemy wanted to make me into someone that was not recognizable. You tried to change me so that God would not remember me. You tried to change His work that He had already put in me. But looking at myself, I am sure that there are so many others that have gone through situations as I did. As I began to testify of my past, I hear so many stories that are like mine.

Your Heart Has a Voice

Sisters of my heart, I see your heart. Your heart has a voice. Your heart wants to speak. But what would it say? I see you, and you see me. Our stories are the same, but we don't know it yet. Your hurt was like mine. I saw you when you saw me. It was like looking into a mirror. When will it all change? My voice is screaming, but I can't be heard. You don't know it yet, but I hear you. You don't know me, but I can hear you. Your eyes are telling your story. Your eyes are speaking for you. We are more alike than you know. Someone has a story like yours. There is an answer. God is your answer. You are His daughter, little girl. He sees you, little girl. He knows where you are, little girl. Use your voice and talk to Him. He wants to know.

It's okay to grieve; you have to because you need to tell your past goodbye. Cry, cry, cry, and then stop. Tell your hurt, "I'm over you. I have no more time for you." Crying, I'm over you so dry up. Shame, I'm over you. You have to go. Now tell the little girl in you that you love her. And that she and I will grow strong together. Discouragement, I'm over you. I'm a winner. Broken heart, I'm over you. I have no place for you in me. So *go*!

Who Took Your Smile?

Where did it go? Did you just forget how? I asked, "Why should I?" What does that mean? I haven't done it in so long, I guess I just forgot. I see people laughing. They laugh because they have glad hearts. Keep it up. There will come a day when I will know what this thing called happiness is all about. I have not been happy for a long time, but I know it's coming. So wait for it.

Blessings in the Rain

There was a day, I don't remember when it was, but there was still a day in my life when I didn't know where you were. I couldn't find you. I couldn't see you move. I couldn't feel the wind blowing. Didn't see anyone walking down my street. Didn't have even a thought. I had but one wish. I wanted to see movement. Even rain would do. I couldn't see anything. It seemed to me that everything was hidden from me. The leaves were still. The trees were still. I saw clouds, but they didn't mean anything to me. I just wished that it would do something. I thought that if it would just rain, then at least I could feel something. It seemed to me that God was even quiet. The air was still. The sun was out, but it was still quiet. I can say, "But God."

One day, He sent some rain. I could see something in the rain. There was rain. I had not seen anything like it. It was raining. I could see it. My vision became clear. I looked at it. It was so precious to me. Just the rain. It was just for me. I felt blessed. I had never seen anything like it. The rain and all of its beauty. I could again see God. I could see me. I came back.

He seemed to say, "The rain has color. The rain has life." He said, "Things are moving. Just look, it's all for you." He gave me back my testimony. He showed me His love. He showed me Him. He said, "Go and tell of my beauty. Somebody needs to know." A little girl is crying because she can't see anything moving. Tell her about the rain so she can see. You have a story. She has someone else's story. Someone else has another story, but they are all the same. The hurt can stop. He or she will not know unless you tell them. You can do it in His love.

I can see beauty again. I could see joy again. Seemed like the Spirit poured back into me. I saw color again. I was no longer in a low place. So He said to me, "Look at this, I did it just for you. You need to know that I love you. You are mine."

Train Up Your Children on Fruits

The spirit of love. I didn't love—only anger, fear, and pain. That was the training I got. The spirit of joy. I never saw joy. I had nothing to be joyful about. The spirit of peace. I got the opposite of peace. There was no calm place for me (Proverbs 2:6). Train up a child in the way he should go, and when he is old, he will not depart from it. And you fathers do not provoke your children to wrath but bring them up in the training and admonition of the Lord (Ephesians 6:4).

He Saw Your Fruit

I t was God who planted the seed in me—the fruit was to be used by Him. It was to grow into something to be used by God alone. He made a place for me. He had a path for me to walk in. He had a calling for my life. God sowed good seed into good ground. He picked the seed He would use for me. But the enemy saw the fruit also. It was pleasant. The enemy doesn't like pleasant. I was supposed to see good in my life. But the enemy covered my eyes with darkness. He said this is play. After all, what child doesn't want to play? And he gave me the opposite of play. He was trying to destroy even the good ground with the good fruit. The good wheat had some tears in it. Where did they come from?

"I'll take away her peace and give her confusion. She has a voice to speak, I'll take that too. If I can take it away from her, then she can't be used by the Holy God." And the story doesn't stop here. You see, I have already won.

I Saw You

Death. You came to take me, but God said not so. I saw you coming, but you couldn't reach me. I didn't see the hand that held you back. I didn't know that it was there. I can look and see now that it was God who stood up for me. I don't know why you didn't let go. For what reason did you keep me here? I can see now that you must have wanted me to know you in the power of your resurrection. You see, I couldn't die unless you said so. Little girl, so sick. I didn't know why, but I was. I could not see any hope for me. I was not old enough to understand hope. I just wanted the pain to stop. I didn't know where I was supposed to go, but I wanted to go. I saw my end. But the end could not reach me. The place that I was in was a place of loneliness, a place of confusion, a place of not having a place to be.

You (enemy) couldn't reach me. I watched you coming for me and still you couldn't come but so close. When the power appeared, and you had to stop, you stood and just watched me. But you couldn't come close enough to touch me. I saw the dark and confused looks on your faces. There were many of you, but you couldn't break through the power. I didn't see you when you left from before me. All I know is you were gone. You have tried to take me out so many times. But God just wouldn't allow it to happen. The power of God was always with me. I didn't know it at the time. I didn't know at that time that I was being protected. I don't even know why.

I remember the time I took those pills and got so sick. I laid down and went to sleep. I don't even know how long I slept or when I woke up. But now that I think about it, the enemy has been trying to stop me for the longest time. And again, the power stood up for me. There must have been a reason. Maybe I have a story to tell. And I can still say I don't know why. So many people are hurting, but so was I. What can I tell them? I know hurt of almost every kind. How can one person know just about every hurt and still be here? I am amazed sometimes at myself. Things I've gone through and yet God bought me out. It must be because of His love.

There is a song that says He keeps doing great things for me. He keeps bringing me out. But when will I start to trust Him with all of my heart? Because God didn't give me a spirit of fear, so what's my problem? I know that God is God and His love is enough for me. Thank for loving me and bringing me out. Lord, if this story needs to be told, I will tell it. Just give me the words in His love.

Why Am I Crying?

Starting to cry, but why? The crying won't stop. Any time. Any day. Any hour. Crying, why are you here? Where are you coming from? Who are you looking for? What do you want? Crying, *stop*! Why are you here? Will you please stop? I don't understand you. I am saved, but I am still crying. I love the Lord, but I am still crying. I thought I had forgotten, but it's that when I hear a song or have a past thought, I am crying. I should be over it, but it won't let me rest. Why am I so sad? What am I doing wrong? I am reading the word of God, and yet I'm still crying. My heart is breaking, and I don't know why.

There came a day when I said that I needed to go and talk to my pastor. As we sat and talked, I told her almost everything that was on my heart. I told her how I was hurting and didn't know why. I just keep crying. And as we talked, she opened up something to me. One of them was that I had never grieved the passing of my mother. She said, "What you are doing is grieving."

I didn't know to grieve. But what did it mean to grieve? I thought I had, but I looked and found out that I never said goodbye. I didn't know to let go. I just wanted to keep her close to me and to say, "Please don't go." I didn't know that I needed to. I didn't remember her face and sill don't. I just remember her. So when I didn't get to look at her in the casket, I didn't really know she was gone.

I thought she had gone away for a little while. I was so afraid that she would one day come back, and I wouldn't recognize, and I didn't want to hurt her anymore. I didn't want her to know that I had forgotten who she was. I was so sorry that I had forgotten her face. At the time I went to my pastor, and I told her what was on my heart. I opened my mouth and began to talk. I saw me as I began to open up.

As I cried, the hurt started to run down my face. I wanted to know what I needed to do. So I cried as she prayed. That's when I saw a miracle. As I cried and prayed to God, I could see Him in my spirit as He stood up. I could see part of His leg. I could see His feet. I could see His hem. I could feel Him as he bent down to me, just because He wanted to hear what I had to say to Him. He wanted to hear my heart. The Lord got so close I could feel His breath as He brushed against my face. His love began to pour into me. I told Him my whole heart, and He listened. He heard my cry.

And so I cried. I forgave my mother for leaving me. I grieved her passing, and I let her go. I saw her as she stood up and she turned and walked out of that broken place that was in me. As she turned, she gave me one more glance, and she walked away.

I could feel the Lord as He began to dig down into the root that kept me bound for so many years, and when He pulled it, it came up—the root and everything around it. I could look down into it in my spirit, and there was nothing left in it—nothing but the peace of God was there. Hanging on to the root was unforgiveness, pain, sadness, loneliness, brokenness, sorrow, confusion, and as the hurt was added to the root, the bigger the hole was getting. To that was added shame, sickness, and blindness. I could see no good in me. I was so angry and hurt. Not really living, just trying to hang on.

"But God." Had it not been for God who was on my side, where would I be? The angry little girl had grown up and became someone I didn't recognize. But I want to say that there is a way out. And that way is in Jesus. He is waiting on you. He is looking and waiting for you. He wants you to know that He loves you and that you are His. All He wants to do is take care of you. He is your father also. He will bring you out, but you have to be ready to come out. You have to be ready to stop crying. For God so loved the world, He gave His only begotten son. He gave Him for you little girl, teenage girl, young women, young mother, and for you, now grandmother and beyond.

If you are still crying, He hears you. Talk to Him; He's listening. I know you have always heard that you should forgive. I say that it's easy to say, but I know that it is not always easy to do. But if you would just give it to Him, He will help you. So if you need to cry for just a little while longer, go ahead. That's okay. Just cry and grieve and then get tired of it. And say, "No more crying, that's it for me."

Tell your hurt to stop. Tell you pain, "You don't belong to me." Tell your voices to *shut up*!

Tell the enemy, "I have no more place for you in my life so *get out*! In the name of Jesus. I'm coming out from under the covers."

Tell the shame, "I am no longer guilty, so you got to go."

Tell the little girl or boy, "I know you still see in your spirit every day. I love you. You are not the blame. And I love you. You can come out. I came to get you. Let's go live."

You still have a long way to go, and you have a long life to live. You have a lot more to do and a lot of places to go. Every bad thing that happened to you will turn out for your good. What the enemy meant for harm has already tuned out for your good.

God who is able to turn things around for you. You are a living testimony. You are sitting on someone's healing. You are on a sick bed that someone else needs. It's time for you to get up. It's time for us to get busy and be about our Father's business. We need to remember that we are not the potter. He is the only one that can put us back together again—all of the hard places, the broken places, the places of discouragement, the place of sadness and loneliness and abuse. He can even fix the "I don't know what to do" next places because God is a father who cares. Even when we ask for forgiveness, He forgives us. And He will. And He will through all of this.

We will still not be perfect, but we know a perfect God. Aren't you tired of the tears? They can get so heavy. They are heavy on your heart, soul, and mind. You know, as I write this, I still have to remind myself that God had to bring me out too. God had brought me out of so many things that you would have to be me to believe it. And the story doesn't end here but the healing does. Even now, I'm still learning to forgive, and I will.

Created for Just a Time as This

I said that I am saved but still not perfect. He lets me know that He loves me, but I'm still not perfect. He said that I can do all things through Him, but I still haven't reached perfection. You were created for such a time as this, so why am I not perfect? You knew that I would mess up, but you still created me for a time like this. You loved me, protected me, showed me the way, gave me your word and your promises. You gave me your son, Jesus. He gave me His life. He rose on the third day just for me. He held back the hand of my enemy and said not so. And after all of this, still I'm not perfect. Yet you created me for just a time like this.

When the Little Heart Hurts

It says in 1 Corinthians 13:11, "When I was a child, I spoke as a child, I understood as a child. My thinking was child-like, but I had to grow up." That's where you come in, my parents. I won't be a child forever so help me to grow. What does that mean?

Hi, little broken heart, what do you want? What can I say to you to make you feel better? What can I say to you to help you heal? Little heart, I see your eyes. What are they saying? My little heart used to ask the question, "Can you see me?" Little heart, I can just bet you have the same question also. How do I come out of this place? Can you hear me? If I scream, will you hear me, or will you just tell me to be quiet? If I scream loud enough, will you turn to me and say, "What is the matter?" Let's see if that will work, so I cry out.

I know if you look at me and just see me, say, "Oh, there you are." Will you hold your arms out and say, "Come here and let me hug you"? Sometimes, that's all I need. Sometimes just look at me. Just look at my eyes and see my heart. I don't want to hurt. I'm trying to call out to you, but you don't hear me. I f I make a sound, you look the other way. I want to say that I love you, but how can I if you won't even look my way? Could it be because you see yourself when you see me? Are you not happy? What can I do or say to help you? I love you, just turn around and look at me. You are here, but I miss you. You bathe me, clothe me, and feed me, but I still miss you. Will you be mine just because you love me?

Sometimes when you are near me, can you just hold my hand? Look, I have hands. I can feel things. I can feel your hands on me so will you just look at me? I can smile. Can you see me?

39

When I'm too quiet, that's when I get lost in plain view. I have to move, play, talk, laugh, even touch you so you won't forget I'm here. Can you see me? What do I look like? What are you thinking about? I can think. I can speak. Will you ask me sometimes what is on my mind? Ask me how I am feeling today. Ask me, "Are you cold? Are you too hot?" or say, "Come here, little one, and give me a hug." Just say something to me from time to time, so that I will know that you see me.

When you don't see me for a while, come and find me. Sometimes I'm lost or hurt, or I just don't understand, so find me. Times when you see me cry, just dry my tears with or without questions. Sometimes I just need a gentle touch. Can you see me? I want you to be glad that I'm here. I want to belong to you. No more hurts, okay? I'm little. It's going to take you to teach me how to grow. So look, I'm still here, and I love you. Little heart with big love.

You see, if you can't see your way to love me, how will I learn to love? If you always shut me out, how will I learn to let others in? If you push me away, that confuses me. When I want to laugh, you tell me to be quiet. When I want to play, you tell me to sit down. But when I'm quiet, that's when you can't see me. Sometimes when I make noise, that's so you don't forget about me. If you make me feel ashamed, that makes me feel guilty. When you speak harsh to me, I won't know how to stand up for myself when it's time for me to go out into this great big world that is all around me. I need to be equipped for this life that I must live. You see, little hurt children will grow into grown-up hurt adults. I know that you are not perfect but watch me so that you will be able to teach me. Remember I belong to you (when I was a child).

About the Author

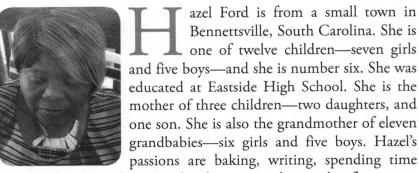

azel Ford is from a small town in Bennettsville, South Carolina. She is one of twelve children—seven girls and five boys—and she is number six. She was educated at Eastside High School. She is the mother of three children—two daughters, and one son. She is also the grandmother of eleven grandbabies—six girls and five boys. Hazel's passions are baking, writing, spending time with her family, cooking Sunday dinners, working in her flower garden, sitting on her porch, enjoying nature, and praying to God. She moved to Charlotte, North Carolina, in 1996 where she met a lot of great people, and she had a lot of great experiences.

In Charlotte was where Hazel found the faith to help build her own home. She also found a great place of worship and the encouragement to begin to write and put her thoughts and feelings on paper. She doesn't know where this adventure will take her, but she is looking for greater things ahead because she found out that it is never too late to go for your dream, and she is definitely ready to go meet her future.